Helping the Environment
Earth-Friendly Eating

by Nick Rebman

www.focusreaders.com

Focus Readers is distributed by North Star Editions:
sales@northstareditions.com | 888-417-0195

Produced for Focus Readers by Red Line Editorial.

Photographs ©: Shutterstock Images, cover, 1, 8, 18, 20–21, 22, 26, 29; iStockphoto, 4, 7, 11, 12, 14, 17; Pixabay, 25

Library of Congress Cataloging-in-Publication Data
Names: Rebman, Nick, author.
Title: Earth-friendly eating / by Nick Rebman.
Description: Lake Elmo, MN : Focus Readers, [2022] | Series: Helping the environment | Includes
   index. | Audience: Grades 2-3
Identifiers: LCCN 2021003719 (print) | LCCN 2021003720 (ebook) | ISBN 9781644938355
   (hardcover) | ISBN 9781644938812 (paperback) | ISBN 9781644939277 (ebook) | ISBN
   9781644939703 (pdf)
Subjects: LCSH: Food--Environmental aspects--Juvenile literature.
Classification: LCC TX357 .R28 2022 (print) | LCC TX357 (ebook) | DDC 641.3--dc23
LC record available at https://lccn.loc.gov/2021003719
LC ebook record available at https://lccn.loc.gov/2021003720

Printed in the United States of America
Mankato, MN
082021

About the Author

Nick Rebman enjoys reading, drawing, and taking long walks with his dog. He lives in Minnesota.

CHAPTER 1

Planning Ahead 5

CHAPTER 2

Problems with Production 9

CHAPTER 3

Working on Solutions 15

THAT'S AMAZING!

Reducing Food Waste 20

CHAPTER 4

How to Help 23

Focus on Earth-Friendly Eating • 28
Glossary • 30
To Learn More • 31
Index • 32

Planning Ahead

A girl and her mother make a shopping list. They figure out what they will need for each meal this week. At the store, they buy only the items on their list.

 Some people write shopping lists on pieces of paper. Others use their phones.

When they get home, it's time to make dinner. First, they boil water and cook some pasta. Next, they fry onions, carrots, and mushrooms. Then, they mix the vegetables into a red sauce. Finally, they add spices to the dish. The meal is a delicious spaghetti dinner for the whole family.

Did You Know?

Making a shopping list helps reduce food waste. It also helps save money.

 The cool temperatures of fridges help keep food from going bad.

When they finish eating, they have leftovers. They put the extra food in the fridge. It will make a great lunch tomorrow. It will also waste less food. The family is eating in an Earth-friendly way.

Chapter 2

Problems with Production

Everyone needs to eat. But food **production** can be harmful to our planet. For example, producing food takes huge amounts of energy. Tractors use energy to plant seeds and gather crops.

 Like many vehicles, tractors burn fossil fuels when they run.

Factories use energy to package food. Trucks use energy to haul food to stores. And stores use energy to keep food fresh.

To create energy, people mainly burn **fossil fuels**. This process releases **greenhouse gases**. These gases cause **climate change**.

Meat uses more energy than other foods. Each year, farmers raise more than 50 billion animals. Those animals burp and fart. This lets greenhouse gases into the air.

Every year, people chop down huge forests in Brazil. Those areas often become cattle ranches.

Animals also drink water and eat food. Farmers use lots of water to grow that food. As a result, other places have little fresh water.

Animals need land to live on, too. People clear forests for room.

The amount of food thrown away around the world could feed more than one billion people.

Forests capture greenhouse gases.

Cutting down forests releases those

gases. And it leaves fewer forests to

capture them.

Certain farming methods are

not Earth-friendly, either. In some

fields, farmers grow only one or two crops. Over time, the soil loses **nutrients**. When that happens, crops take more energy to grow.

Another huge problem is food waste. People throw away nearly one-third of all food. But all that food still took lots of energy to produce.

Did You Know?

Approximately 30 percent of the world's energy is used on food production.

Chapter 3

Working on Solutions

People have come up with many ways to make food more Earth-friendly. For example, people designed tractors and trucks that use less fuel. They also made refrigerators that use less energy.

 Certain chemicals help fridges cool. Those chemicals can have a larger climate impact than fossil fuels.

Another way is to cut down on eating meat. Some places are serving less meat. Examples include hospitals and schools.

Eating less meat has another **benefit**. It decreases the amount of land needed for farms. So, people do not have to clear as many forests.

Changes to animals' diets can help the planet, too. For example, certain foods reduce the amount of greenhouse gases cows produce.

Some cultures have many meat-free dishes. This Indian lentil-and-spinach dish is one example.

Many farms are also using less water. Some farmers no longer use sprinklers. Instead, they use machines that send drips of water directly to each plant's roots. That way, less water **evaporates**.

Farmers can raise farm animals along with forests. This practice helps avoid clearing trees.

Some farmers work on improving the soil. For example, they plant several different crops in each field. As a result, the soil does not lose nutrients.

In addition, governments have created messages about food waste. That way, more people know about the problem. Restaurants, schools, and grocery stores have also tried to cut down on waste. For instance, they may give extra food to people in need.

Did You Know?

Some plant-based foods taste similar to meat. But they take far less energy to produce.

Reducing Food Waste

Food waste is a big problem in schools. At one school, a group of students took action. They set up tables in the lunchroom. People could leave food they did not want. Then other people could take the food. The idea worked. Less food ended up in the trash.

The students made a video, too. They talked about ways to reduce food waste. They showed the video to other students. People took notice. The school reduced food waste by more than 25 percent.

Increasing school lunchtimes can help reduce food waste.

Chapter 4

How to Help

You can do many things to make your food more Earth-friendly. One important thing is reducing food waste. Make sure you actually eat the food you buy. Planning your meals is a great way to do this.

 If people bought only what they would eat, food waste would drop.

You can also eat foods that don't use lots of water or energy. In general, plant-based meals are more Earth-friendly. If you eat meat, choose more chicken and turkey. These meats use less energy than beef.

Some plants use more water than others. Seeds use less water than nuts, for example. Beans are also good choices. Certain seafoods are also Earth-friendly. They include oysters and clams.

 Beans are an Earth-friendly food that provide similar nutrients to meat.

Each person can make a small difference. There are also ways to make an even bigger difference.

 Talking to school leaders, such as teachers and principals, can lead to school-wide changes.

You can ask larger groups to take action. For example, you can talk to your school's principal. Ask about having more plant-based meals. You can also start a group focused on food waste.

   Writing to lawmakers is another way to make a difference. Lawmakers can make stronger rules about energy use and water use. They can also spread awareness about food waste.

Did You Know?

Plant-based diets tend to be healthier than meat-based diets.

FOCUS ON
Earth-Friendly Eating

Write your answers on a separate piece of paper.

1. Write a paragraph that describes the main ideas of Chapter 3.

2. Should governments encourage people to eat more plant-based meals? Why or why not?

3. How can farmers improve their soil?
   A. They can plant several different kinds of crops in each field.
   B. They can increase the number of animals that they raise.
   C. They can stop using sprinklers to water their crops.

4. What is one way to reduce food waste?
   A. Burn fewer fossil fuels.
   B. Eat more plant-based meals.
   C. Save leftovers for the next day.

5. What does **capture** mean in this book?

*Forests **capture** greenhouse gases. Cutting down forests releases those gases.*

    A. chop down

    B. take in

    C. give out

6. What does **designed** mean in this book?

*For example, people **designed** tractors and trucks that use less fuel. They also made refrigerators that use less energy.*

    A. made plans for

    B. drove slowly

    C. kept something cold

Answer key on page 32.

Glossary

benefit
A good result that happens after doing a certain thing.

climate change
A human-caused global crisis involving long-term changes in Earth's temperature and weather patterns.

evaporates
Changes from liquid to gas.

fossil fuels
Energy sources that come from the remains of plants and animals that died long ago.

greenhouse gases
Gases in the air that trap heat from the sun.

nutrients
Substances that humans, animals, and plants need to stay strong and healthy.

production
The process of making something.

To Learn More

BOOKS

Burling, Alexis. *Turning Poop into Power.* Minneapolis: Abdo Publishing, 2020.

Kurtz, Kevin. *The Future of Food.* Minneapolis: Lerner Publications, 2021.

McCarthy, Cecilia Pinto. *Eating Bugs as Sustainable Food.* Minneapolis: Abdo Publishing, 2020.

NOTE TO EDUCATORS

Visit **www.focusreaders.com** to find lesson plans, activities, links, and other resources related to this title.

Index

C

crops, 9, 13, 18

F

farmers, 10–11, 13, 17–18
food waste, 6–7, 13, 19,
   20, 23, 27
forests, 11–12, 16

G

greenhouse gases, 10,
   12, 16

L

lawmakers, 27
leftovers, 7

M

meat, 10, 16, 19, 24, 27

P

plant-based foods, 19,
   24, 27

S

schools, 16, 19, 20, 26
shopping list, 5–6
soil, 13, 18

Answer Key: 1. Answers will vary; **2.** Answers will vary; **3.** A; **4.** C; **5.** B; **6.** A